NATIVE AMERICAN ART

Petra Press

Heinemann Library
Chicago, Illinois

Customer Service 888-454-2279

Visit our website at www.heinemannlibrary.com

Printed in China

05 04 03 02 01
10 9 8 7 6 5 4 3 2 1

Library of Congress Cataloging-in-Publication Data
Press, Petra.
 Native American art / Petra Press.
   p. cm. -- (Art in history)
Includes bibliographical references and index.
 ISBN 1-58810-092-8 (lib. bdg.)
 1. Indian art--North America--Juvenile literature. [1. Indian art--North America.] I. Title. II. Series: Art in history (Chicago, Ill.)
E98.A7 P74 2001
704.03'97--dc21
                              00-012481

Acknowledgments
© Corbis/David Muench, Cover; © Art Resource/Werner Forman, 5; © Corbis/Morton Beebe, S.F., 6; © Corbis/Buddy Mays, 7; © Corbis/Richard Hamilton Smith, 8; © Corbis/David Muench, 9; © American Museum Natural History/Neg./Transparency No. 319175. Courtesy Department of Library Services, 10; © National Museum of American Art/Smithsonian American Art Museum, Gift of Mrs. Joseph Harrison, Jr., 11; © Corbis/Richard A Cooke, 12; © Art Resource/Werner Forman Archive, Private Collection, 13; © Brooklyn Museum/"Panther Effigy Pipe", USA, Indiana, AD 1-4000 Black steatite 6.0 x 17.t x 4.0 cm, Anonymous loan L49.5, 14; © Ohio Historical Society, 15; © Art Resource/The Newark Museum, Newark, New Jersey, 16; © Art Resource/Werner Forman Archive, Museum of Anthropology, University of British Columbia, Canada, 17; © National Museum of the American Indian, 18; © Portland Art Museum/Portland Art Museum, Portland, Oregon, Axel Rasmussen Collection, purchased with the Indian Collection Subscription Fund, 19; © Corbis/Richard A Cooke, 20; © Corbis/David Muench, 21; © National Museum of the American Indian/Courtesy, National Museum of the American Indian, Smithsonian Institution (Neg# 15/0855) Photo by David Heald, 22; © Art Resource/Werner Forman Archive, British Museum, London, 23; © Corbis/Ted Spiegel, 24; © Corbis/Buddy Mays, 25; © Photo Researchers, Inc./Georg Gerster, 26; © Saint Louis Art Musuem/Eliza McMillan Fund, 27; © Bernice Steinbaum Gallery/Jeff Sturges, 28

Some words are shown in bold, **like this.**
You can find out what they mean by looking in the glossary.

CONTENTS

WHAT IS NATIVE AMERICAN ART?

Native American cultures have existed in North America for thousands of years. Over 500 different Native American nations were spread over seven major ecological areas, which are sometimes called **culture areas.** These areas are now called the Northwest Pacific Coast, California, Basin Plateau, Southwest, Great Plains, Southeast, and Eastern Woodlands. Each of these nations has a rich culture that is thousands of years old, and includes history, government, religion, and myths.

Communities of Native North Americans developed artistic skills to express their beliefs and history in a variety of ways, just as people did in other parts of the world. The beautiful objects the Native Americans created always had a social or religious use. Creating art and practicing religion were part of everyday life, since **functional** objects were designed to remind people of their beliefs, their traditions, and their history.

This map shows the different culture areas in North America.

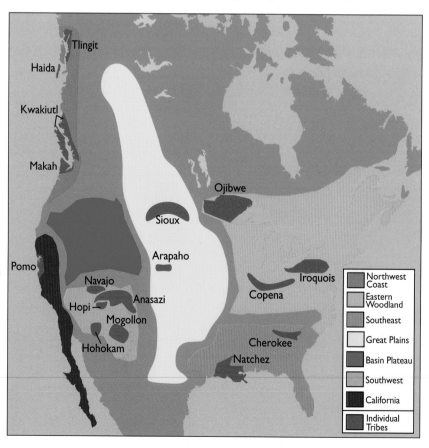

Each culture developed a unique and recognizable style, although neighboring communities often traded skills and materials. Everyone created functional art objects, but in every area there were specialists, since some people were more skilled than others. Whether it was carving a **ceremonial** pipe, weaving a basket or blanket, or painting a battle scene on a rock wall, each artist worked with great care so that the object would contribute to the harmony and beauty of the world.

Lakota Sioux painting on buckskin.

Paintings like this one were often done to show the owner's skill in battle. The paintings were also used as historical documents for people to find out about their history and heroes.

New tools and designs

Until the arrival of Europeans, Native Americans used painstaking traditional techniques to create their functional and ceremonial art objects. The Europeans introduced chemical dyes, the potter's wheel, metalworking, and the sewing needle, making it easier for Native Americans to produce some of their art. Europeans had a negative impact as well. Early European settlers wanted to trade for Native American pottery, baskets, and textiles but thought the designs were primitive. Over the years, many Native American artists began to change the color, shape, and size of their creations to meet the demand of white traders.

SIGNS AND SYMBOLS

While no two Native American cultures developed exactly the same religion, most agreed that spirits lived in the animals, rocks, rivers, land, and trees around them. Every being had a soul that had to be respected. When a hunter killed a deer for food, he thanked the animal for its **sacrifice** and then buried its bones so that its spirit could be reborn.

Native Americans believed that all life should be in harmony with its environment. **Shamans** held rituals to call on certain spirits to heal sickness and to protect the community from its enemies. Shamans carved and painted special masks, pipes, **rattles,** and **amulets** in the shapes of the spirits whose help they needed. Tlingit shamans in the Northwest Pacific Coast **culture area** asked the sea otter for help, while shamans in the Plains culture area called on the buffalo.

Totem pole, Kwakiutl people, British Columbia, cedar wood.

Totem poles were carved from one large tree trunk. Each animal spirit carved on the pole had a specific meaning and importance for the owner.

Other tribe members carved amulets that they carried for protection against enemies and sickness. Often the person also carried an amulet in the shape of his or her animal spirit. The animal spirits and natural world are important symbols in Native American art.

Teenage boys spent months preparing for a **vision quest,** a **spiritual** event that sent the teenager on a long hike away from the village with no food and water. The teenager would stay away from the village until an animal came to him in a dream. He then took the animal spirit's name, such as Running Deer or Spotted Eagle, as his own, and returned to the village as an adult. Bears, deer, wolves, birds, and frogs all served as animal spirits.

Kachina, Hopi people, Arizona, wood.

The Hopi believe that each kachina carving can pass on some of the power of the kachina spirit it represents.

Kachinas
Hopi dancers wore carved and painted wooden masks in a ceremony to thank spirits they called kachinas for a bountiful harvest. Small kachina dolls were intricately carved in one piece of wood or one piece of the root of a cotton plant, then brightly painted. Kachinas were given to babies as amulets to bring them good health and a long life.

ROCK ART

Rock art, the pictures painted or carved on rocks or cave walls, was used to record battles, history, and other important tribal events. Some cultures used it to tell religious stories. Over 2,500 years ago, the Anasazi Indians of the Southwest **culture area** painted human figures called **pictographs** on the sandstone rock of desert canyons, and the Great Plains people painted pictographs in the Midwest, near the Great Lakes. Painted in bright yellows and reds, the pictures showed people hunting animals or fighting each other. Many showed people playing flutes and other musical instruments. The most common paintings are red and white hand prints of children and adults, believed to have been placed there during religious ceremonies.

Pictograph, Hegman Lake, Minnesota, red paint on rock.

This pictograph shows a hunter with his prey.

Petroglyphs

The rock art found throughout the rest of North America was created over a thousand years later. In addition to pictograph paintings of animal spirits, some cultures used a different kind of rock art, called **petroglyphs.** Petroglyphs were images or a sort of picture alphabet carved into rock to record a tribe's history, to serve as a symbol in important ceremonies, or to make detailed maps of hunting locations. These forms of rock art are important, because by examining them we can learn a lot about the way people used to live.

Petroglyph, Wind River Range, Wyoming, carving on rock.

*This figure was probably carved by a **shaman** in a ceremony to ensure a successful hunt.*

USING TREES AND PLANTS

Native Americans of the Eastern Woodlands **culture area** used the bark of white birch trees to make hundreds of useful objects. It was light, easy to work with, waterproof, and didn't rot in hot weather, so it was perfect for constructing canoes and covering **wigwams.** People also made storage containers out of it, and used it to make hunting and fishing gear, musical instruments, decorative fans, and even children's sleds and other toys. Birch bark was also used to write on, since it is durable and light enough to be carried around.

Records, Ojibwe people, birch bark, ca. seventeenth century

*These records are easily readable, even after being handled by many people. They were made by Ojibwe people who were part of the Midewiwin group. This was a secret society of **shamans.** It was formed to protect people from new diseases that had been brought by the white settlers. The members kept notes about their meetings on birch bark.*

Portrait of an Iroquois
Wife, *George Catlin, ca. 1835.*

*This Iroquois woman
has made a cradle for her
baby using branches and
plant fibers.*

Native Americans also used the roots and twigs of willow, spruce, and pine trees, as well as plants such as cattails and corn husks to create household objects, bows and arrows, children's toys and cradles, and **ceremonial** masks and **rattles.** Plant fibers could easily be bent into many different shapes. Using plant fibers gave the finished objects interesting textures and colors.

WOOD SCULPTURE

Wood carving was especially popular along the Northwest Pacific Coast **culture area** where large planks were cut from trees to construct houses big enough to hold dozens of people. People built canoes that were large enough to hunt whales out on the ocean, and carved tall poles decorated with their family's **totems** and guardian animal spirits. They carved helmets, shields, and clubs to use in battle. Almost all of their carved objects, whether large or small, were richly painted. Paint was made from bark, berries, and moss. The artist painted the carving using a paintbrush made of porcupine hair.

*Carved wood **rattle**, Makah people, Washington.*

Rattles like this one were used in religious ceremonies or to emphasize parts of important speeches.

The potlach
Northwest Pacific Coast peoples were able to store enough of the food that they hunted, fished, and gathered in the summers that they could devote their winters to throwing elaborate feasts and parties called **potlatches**. It was traditional to give each of one's guests a beautifully carved or woven gift. The more elaborate the gifts, the higher one's status in the community. The gifts were often ornately carved serving bowls or intricately designed blankets.

Wood carving was much more developed in the Eastern Woodlands and Northwest Pacific Coast culture areas because fewer trees grew in the deserts of the Southwest. People living in and near forests used wood for just about everything, including tool handles, containers to store food and clothing, ceremonial masks and rattles, serving bowls, and utensils such as spoons and corn flatteners. These items were often carved in the shapes of beavers, hawks, snakes, and other animals.

In the Southeast culture area, mask carving was a highly developed specialty. The Cherokee carved cougar masks for ceremonies to honor the cougar and to give the hunters cat-like hunting abilities. They also carved masks for ceremonies like the Boogerman Dance, a dance that was performed to scare away evil spirits that tried to harm their crops. They painted and decorated the wooden masks with animal fur, quills, feathers, toenails, and even teeth.

Mask of a beaver and killer whale, Kwakiutl people, British Columbia, ca. 1700 C.E.

Masks like this one were used in elaborate ceremonial dances. Kwakiutl masks had parts that could move for more dramatic ceremonies.

STONE SCULPTURE

Native North Americans used stone as well as wood to carve objects such as bowls, farming tools, **ceremonial** figures, and arrowheads. Tools made out of harder rock were used to carve soft rock such as **limestone,** soapstone, and catlinite. Limestone was used for larger statues because it is less heavy than other types of rock. Soapstone, so named because it feels like soap, was popular for smaller projects, such as pipes and bowls, because it is soft and easily carved. Catlinite, also known as **pipestone,** is a special form of hard red clay that worked well for burning tobacco in the stems and bowls of ceremonial pipes. Some important pipes were called **effigy pipes.** These pipes came in all sizes and animal shapes, although cats and other graceful animals were popular subjects. Some pipes were for everyday use, but most effigy pipes were used for ceremonies and rituals.

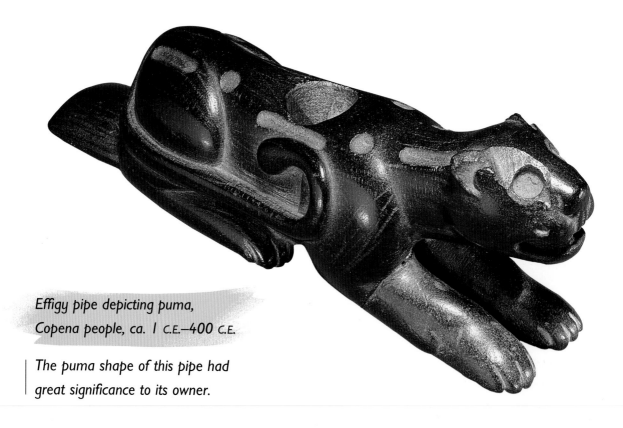

Effigy pipe depicting puma, Copena people, ca. 1 C.E.–400 C.E.

The puma shape of this pipe had great significance to its owner.

After the Europeans introduced metal tools to North America, some Native Americans, such as the Haida of the Northwest Pacific Coast **culture area,** started carving boxes and other objects out of harder rocks such as argulite and black shale. In addition to animal designs, such as the raven and whale, people carved their first impressions of the European traders and settlers who landed on their coasts.

Platform effigy pipe in the shape of a frog, Copena people, ca. 1 C.E.–400 C.E.

This effigy pipe is carved from catlinite, which is often called pipestone. It was used during important ceremonies.

Metals
Native North American artists did not use much metal until the Europeans introduced new ways to refine iron, gold, and silver in the sixteenth century. Copper was the only metal they used before then. Some cultures in the Northwest Pacific Coast culture area pounded copper into thin decorative plates that they gave as gifts at the elaborate **potlatch** parties they threw each winter.

BASKETRY

Native Americans in the Great Plains and the Southwest were weaving baskets over 11,000 years ago. The Anasazi, **ancestors** of the Pueblo people in the Southwest **culture area,** used baskets for everything from baby cradles to funeral jars. They also used baskets to gather and store food. Bowl-shaped baskets were woven so tightly that they were waterproof. These baskets were used as hats, or to transport water, and could also be used to cook food.

Pomo ceremonial gift basket, Pomo people, California, willow, feathers, abalone shells, ca. nineteenth century.

During the nineteenth century, the Pomo people made coiled baskets like this one to sell to white settlers in California. They sold the baskets to raise money so they could buy back their land from the white settlers.

Weaving and coiling

There were two major ways of making baskets: weaving and coiling. Both ways used all kinds of grasses, roots, bark, and other plant materials. Weaving—pulling softer fibers in and out of stiffer fibers that formed the basic basket shape—produced the strongest baskets. Coiling—wrapping a long, thick strand of fiber around and around and then sewing the coils together—was a faster method, but not as sturdy. Finished baskets were often decorated with animal designs or tribal symbols. Plant dyes were used to color the materials shades of red, yellow, black, purple, green-blue, brown, and white. Weavers often decorated the finished baskets with feathers, quills, shells, leather, or beads. Size varied from small **trinket** baskets to four-foot-high storage jars that could take as long as two years to make.

Basket with killer whale design, Tlingit people, Alaska, woven spruce root.

Baskets like this one were useful as well as beautiful. This basket is woven, not coiled.

TEXTILES

Fabric weaving is a lot like basket weaving, since it consists of threading strips of one material over and under stiffer strips of another. However, preparing the materials is difficult, and it took thousands of years longer to evolve. By 700 C.E., the Anasazi had developed a simple upright loom, a large square made of wooden poles that held the stiffer fibers in place. The cloth that they wove from cactus fiber and hemp plants resembles the cotton that is woven today. It was used to make blankets, **serapes,** shawls, shoes, and bags. Because **sacred** symbols and designs were woven into the fabrics, weaving was considered a sacred occupation. Women, and in some cultures, men, were considered the weavers of the thread of life.

Navajo blanket, Navajo people, Arizona, wool.

Navajo blankets are still woven on looms made by the weaver.

Weaving materials

In addition to plant fibers, weavers used feathers and the fur of animals such as rabbits and dogs. Weaving of wool did not begin until the Spanish introduced sheep into the Southwest **culture area** around 1600 C.E. Other popular sources of weaving materials that were used after Europeans started settling the continent were the old uniforms, army blankets, and red flannel underwear that white settlers traded to Native Americans. The Native Americans unraveled these items and redyed the wool before weaving it into their own designs to make blankets and clothing.

Chilkat weave shirt, Tlingit people, Alaska, cedar bark and mountain goat wool weave with fur lining.

The chilkat weave symbolized wealth. Sometimes wealthy people burned these shirts and robes as proof of their wealth and status.

POTTERY

The first **nomadic** Native Americans used lightweight baskets to gather and store food. Pottery developed much later, when people discovered that if they smeared baskets with clay and then dried them, they would hold water. By the year 200 B.C.E., the Hohokam people of the Southwest **culture area** were molding bowls and jars out of wet clay. Potters' wheels didn't exist until Europeans introduced them in the sixteenth century. Instead, a potter would use the bottom of a broken pot to form the base of a new one. He or she rolled coils of clay to form the walls of the bowl or jug, then pinched the coils together, shaped the pot with tools made from gourds or sticks, and smoothed it with water. The pottery was hardened over an outdoor fire, often using dried animal dung for fuel.

Pottery, Anasazi people, Mesa Verde, Colorado, ca. 600 C.E.–1300 C.E.

This pottery was found in Mesa Verde, an Anasazi city built high on the cliffs of Colorado.

Pottery also played a major role in religious ceremonies and rituals. When **archaeologists** excavated the Mogollon people's burial sites in the Mimbres area, they discovered skeletal remains with clay bowls covering the heads. Magical images of clouds, animals, and spirits were painted on the interiors of each bowl. Each bowl had a hole in the bottom so the person's spirit could escape.

By 700 C.E., people in the Southwest culture area were painting their pottery in striking black and white designs. The artists chewed the ends of twigs to make their brushes. They also began making small, animal-shaped **ceremonial** figures and pipes out of clay. Over time, individual villages became known for their different pot shapes and decorative styles, which included animal and insect shapes and geometric patterns. Yellow and red became the traditional colors in some areas, while some cultures continued to use black and white.

With the exception of some parts of the Northwest Pacific Coast culture area, pottery developed all over North America, although it was never as beautifully shaped and painted in other places as it was in the Southwest.

Pot with bat, Mogollon people, Gila Cliff Dwellings, New Mexico, ca. 950–1350 C.E.

This pot was made to be used in a burial. We can tell that it was never used, since it does not have a hole in the bottom.

JEWELRY AND HEADDRESSES

Many Native North Americans wore some type of jewelry or other body decoration to show that they belonged to a certain **clan** or tribe. The jewelry was often a tooth, claw, or other animal part carried as a **totem,** or it was an **amulet,** hair ornament, or necklace made out of beads, shells, or feathers. Such items were often given to teenagers to celebrate their passage into adulthood after their **vision quest,** or to young men when they became warriors. Beads and feathers also decorated clothing worn to celebrate weddings or other special ceremonies. Necklaces made of shells were worn to prevent illness, while **shamans** often wore red face paint and red hair ornaments to cure a sickness.

Disk with crested woodpeckers, shell, ca. 1250–1300 C.E.

This disk was carved to decorate a necklace. The woodpeckers carved on it would have had great importance for the owner.

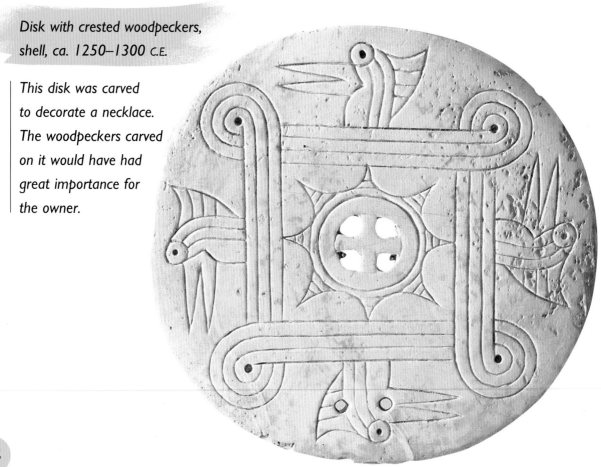

Native Americans added glass beads to their jewelry and clothing designs after Europeans introduced them to North America in the sixteenth century. In some cultures, men and women wore **wampum** beads to show they were important tribal members. The beads were also used as money to trade for other goods.

Many Native American cultures also came to be known for their featherwork. People wore feathers as jewelry or on clothing and headdresses to mark their social status, and some feathers were worn in **spiritual** ceremonies. One common belief was that a feather represented the qualities of the bird it came from. Cherokee tribes considered owl, hummingbird, eagle, turkey, and buzzard feathers particularly powerful. They believed that owl feathers represented wisdom, while eagle feathers represented honor and success.

War bonnet, Arapaho people, eagle feathers, shells, beads, and leather.

War bonnets like this one were worn by tribes that lived on the Plains. This bonnet is fairly short. Some of them had feathers that reached all the way down to the wearer's knees!

SANDPAINTINGS

According to Navajo legend, Holy People animate all things, including animals, people, trees, winds, rivers, even colors, and the four directions. The Holy People teach about the harmony of the universe. The Navajo believe that to keep the Holy People happy, everything must be kept in balance. When a Navajo is sick or has misfortune, it is because bad spirits have entered his or her body, and he or she has thrown the balance of the universe out of harmony. To regain health or fortune, the person must ask an *Hatathli,* which means "singer" in Navajo, to conduct a long and complex healing ceremony. An important part of this ceremony is the creation of sandpaintings.

This modern Navajo shaman is creating a sandpainting for a healing ceremony.

The Singer is the Navajo **shaman.** He or she uses colored sand to create a **sacred** design on a large piece of **buckskin.** Then, the sick person is purified with sweat baths. This means that he or she is placed in a small covered place where a fire is burning, so it is full of steam. The steam makes the person sweat all of the bad things out of his or her body. After this, he or she kneels in the middle of the painting, facing east, and prays, often for days at a time, while the Singer chants. The colors white, blue, yellow, and black symbolize dawn, daylight, twilight, and night. The singer draws the spirits of animals and draws plants, such as corn, beans, squash, and tobacco, that have special healing powers. When the healing ritual is over, the painting is swept away. The healing ceremony and sandpainting are ancient traditions. They have been important ceremonies in the Navajo culture for hundreds of years.

Sandpainting of a Yei God, Navajo shaman, western New Mexico, colored sand, ca. 1985–1995 C.E.

Yei gods, like the one in this painting, are summoned by shamans to cure a sick person by pushing the bad spirits out of his or her body.

Bear Sickness

The Navajo believe that feeling faint, nervousness, and troubled memory are all symptoms of a condition called bear sickness. This sickness can be caused by eating bear meat, killing a bear, or dreaming about a bear. To cure bear sickness, the shaman makes a sandpainting and performs a ceremony called the Mountain Chant, or Mountaintop Way.

EARTH MOUNDS

Some of the most impressive Native American creations archaeologists have discovered are the more than 100,000 **earth mounds** found throughout the Eastern Woodlands **culture area** and in the Ohio and Mississippi River Valleys. Many are small, simple mounds, but others are monumental works of art, built in the shape of birds or animals. Some are as large as the Great Pyramids of Egypt and can only be fully appreciated when they are viewed from the air. The Great Serpent Mound in Ohio is 1,348 ft. long, 20 ft. wide, and 2.6 ft. high (410 m long, 6 m wide, and 80 cm high).

Great Serpent Mound, Adena people, sculpted mound of earth and rock, near Locust Grove, Ohio, ca. 100 B.C.E. to 700 C.E.

Some scientists think that the serpent mound was designed as a ceremonial calendar.

It is likely that the mounds were built over a span of several thousand years, from about 700 B.C.E. to about 1500 C.E. by three main farming cultures: the Adena, the Hopewell, and the Mississippian, also called the Natchez. Most were built as burial monuments and had a central chamber that contained the remains of important tribal members. Others were cemetery plots for less important people, often containing 50 or more separately buried bodies. New mounds were often built on top of older ones from previous generations.

Objects that were buried with the dead, including pottery, **effigy pipes,** and tools, were often made from materials such as copper, seashells, and certain kinds of stone that were not readily available in the Eastern Woodlands. This tells **archaeologists** that the mound-building cultures must have conducted trade over great distances with people from other culture areas.

Panorama of the Monumental Grandeur of the Mississippi Valley, *John J. Egan, ca. 1850 C.E.*

This painting shows archaeologists studying an earth mound in the Mississippi River valley.

NATIVE AMERICAN PAINTING

For thousands of years, Native artists painted rocks, pottery, and leather objects with images that reflected their **spiritual** beliefs, community history, and pride. In the nineteenth and early twentieth centuries, Native Americans were forced to give up their culture so they could blend into white America, and many Native American art forms disappeared. By the 1950s, institutions such as the Institute of American Indian Art began to encourage Native American artists to go back and relearn their traditional art forms. Today, the nation's most important artists include Native Americans like Juane Quick-to-See Smith. These modern artists are using traditional and **sacred** art forms to express new ideas.

Herd, *Juane Quick-to-See Smith,*
1998.

In this painting, Smith has drawn outlines of a traditional image, the buffalo, over a collage made of articles and pictures that illustrate the selfish qualities of modern society.

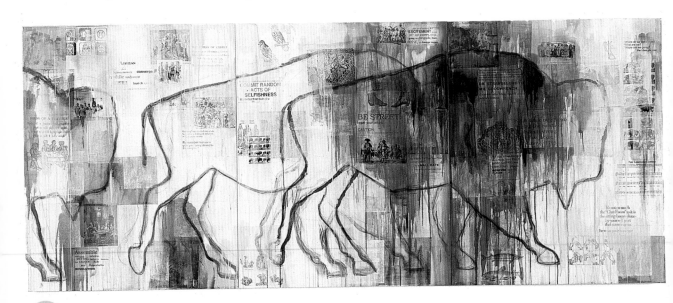

Make a Buckskin Painting

You will need:

paper grocery bag with the bottom cut off and the side cut to make a rectangle

crayons in colors like brown, orange, red, black, and yellow

newspapers

an iron

black permanent marker

household wax

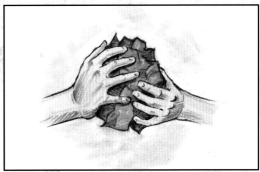

1. Use the crayons to draw an image on the grocery bag. Use the painting on page 5 for guidance. When your drawing is done, rub household wax in all the areas of the bag that are not covered in crayon.

2. Crush the bag with your picture on it into a ball, then open it up again. Repeat this about twenty times to make your picture look old and wrinkled. You can even step on the ball to make the wrinkles deeper.

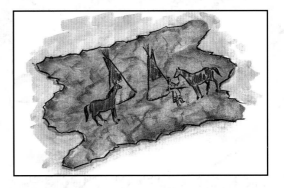

3. Put your open picture between two layers of newspaper. Have an adult help you iron the newspaper above your picture until the wax begins to melt through the newspaper.

4. Remove your picture from the newspaper, and go over the outlines in black permanent marker. Cut the picture into the shape of an animal hide. Your picture should have the wrinkled look and soft feel of a real buckskin painting.

TIMELINE

B.C.E.

50,000 to 15,000	The first migration across the Bering Strait brings people to North America.
10,000	The first stone arrowheads are carved in the Great Plains.
9000	Basketry and early woodcarving are developed throughout North America.
4000	Early weaving techniques are developed and used to make baskets.
2000	Painted pottery develops in the Southwest.
500	The Anasazi and Plains people start creating rock art.
700	Cultures in the Eastern Woodlands culture area and Ohio and Mississippi River Valleys start building earth mounds.

C.E.

1492	Columbus establishes the first European colony in North America.
1500s	Europeans introduce the potter's wheel, the upright loom, beads, and metal work to some Native American cultures.
1800s	Congress passes the Indian Removal Act, forcing Native Americans onto reservations.
1880–1890s	U.S. troops in the West kill many Native Americans who are fighting to keep their land.
1940	Juane Quick-to-See Smith is born.
1950s	Native American artists relearn old pottery, weaving, carving, and basketry skills as a result of the founding of the Institute of American Indian Art.
1989	The National Museum of the American Indian is established by an act of Congress.
1990	The Indian Arts and Crafts Act is passed, and all authentic Native American art is certified.

GLOSSARY

amulet ornament carried to protect the wearer

ancestor person you are related to from the past, such as your grandmother

archaeologist person who studies the past using objects made by people in the past

buckskin tanned deer hide used to make clothing, tents, and other objects

ceremonial used in a ritual

clan group of people with something in common, who usually live together

culture areas region of the U.S. where there were several Native American groups that shared beliefs and customs

earth mound massive burial sites that were often built in animal shapes

effigy pipe pipe carved to resemble a person or animal spirit

functional made to use in everyday living, or as part of religious ceremonies

limestone soft stone that is easy to carve

nomadic tending to move from place to place

petroglyph pictures carved into rock to tell a story

pictograph painting on rock

pipestone soft, red stone, also called catlinite, that was used to make pipes

potlach elaborate feast common in the Northwest Pacific Coast area

rattle musical instrument that makes noise when it is shaken

sacred highly respected or worshiped

sacrifice losing or giving away something important for the good of others

serape woven cape worn over the shoulder

shaman Native American religious leader who can communicate with the spirits

spirituality having to do with religion

totem animal spirit used as a family symbol and as personal protection

trinket small object

vision quest spiritual journey made by young Native Americans to mark the change from child to adult

wampum beads made of shells or other valuable materials that were worn and also used as money

wigwam round shelter made of poles covered with bark or hides

MORE BOOKS TO READ

Innes, Brian. *Native American Monuments.* Austin, Tex.: Raintree Steck-Vaughn, 1999.

La Pierre, Yvette. *Native American Rock Art: Messages from the Past.* West Palm Beach, Fla.: Lickle Publishing, Inc., 1994.

Moore, Reavis and LaVar Burton. *Native Artists of North America.* Emeryville, Calif.: Avalon Travel Publishing, 1993.

Wood, Marion. *Ancient America.* New York: Facts on File, 1990.

INDEX